WHAT WE CAN DO ABOUT

RECYCLING RUBBISH

Donna Bailey

Franklin Watts

London   New York   Sydney   Toronto

Original text © 1991 Donna Bailey
© 1991 Zoe Books Limited

Devised and produced by
Zoe Books Limited
15 Worthy Lane
Winchester
Hampshire SO23 7AB
England

First published in 1991
in Great Britain by
Franklin Watts Ltd
96 Leonard Street
London EC2A 4RH

First published in Australia by
Franklin Watts Australia
14 Mars Road
Lane Cove
New South Wales 2066

ISBN 0 7496 0407 7

A CIP catalogue record for this book is available from the British Library.

Printed in Italy

Design: Julian Holland Publishing Ltd
Illustrator: Martin Smillie
Picture researcher: Alison Renwick

Photograph acknowledgements
t = top *b* = bottom
Cover: Chris Fairclough Colour Library
pp3 Alcan Aluminium Ltd, 6 Chris Fairclough Colour Library, 7 David Goulston/
Bruce Coleman Ltd, 8 R Dorel/Robert Harding Picture Library, 9 *t* Chris
Fairclough Colour Library, 9*b* Ian Griffiths/Robert Harding Picture Library, 10
Jimmy Holmes/The Environmental Picture Library, 11 Chris Fairclough Colour
Library, 12 Jimmy Holmes/The Environmental Picture Library, 13*t* Jack Dermid/
Bruce Coleman Ltd, 13*b* Philip Carr/The Environmental Picture Library, 14 Jimmy
Holmes/The Environmental Picture Library, 15 S & R Greenhill, 16 Alcan
Aluminium Ltd, 17 Warren Spring Laboratory, 18 C B & D W Frith/Bruce
Coleman Ltd, 19*t* John Lythgage/Planet Earth Pictures, 19*b* Mark Boulton/ICCE
Photolibrary, 20, 21, 22, 23*t*, 23*b* Chris Fairclough Colour Library, 24 Alex
Williams/Greenpeace Communications Ltd, 25 Barry Waddams, 26 Chris
Fairclough Colour Library, 27 Topham Picture Source.

Contents

What a lot of rubbish

Have you ever looked inside your rubbish bin? Most of our rubbish is a mixture of many different kinds of things. There may be glass bottles, plastic bottles, plastic bags, newspapers, metal cans and vegetable peelings.

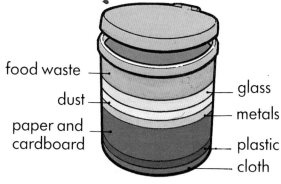

food waste
dust
paper and cardboard
glass
metals
plastic
cloth

The average amounts of different materials in a typical rubbish bin.

Every year, each household throws away about one **tonne** of rubbish. If you think how many **households** there are in the country and add together all their rubbish, it comes to a huge amount. Then there is the rubbish from factories, shops, restaurants and farms. We have to get rid of all this rubbish somehow.

Most household rubbish is dumped in large holes, such as old **quarries**. Some rubbish is burnt. Both these ways of getting rid of rubbish can cause problems such as **pollution**. It would be less wasteful if we could reuse rubbish or make new things from it. This is known as **recycling**.

Bury it or burn it?

In most towns and cities, we put our rubbish into bins. Rubbish collectors come with dustcarts to collect our rubbish. They put the bins on to mechanical lifts, which empty the rubbish into the cart. Some pieces of rubbish are too big to go in the bins and so the rubbish collectors have to heave these items into the dustcart themselves.

Inside the dustcart the rubbish is squashed, to take up as little space as possible. The rubbish is then taken to a rubbish dump, or **landfill site**. Sometimes the dustcarts travel a long way every day to the landfill site, because suitable sites nearer the towns soon get filled up.

At the landfill site the rubbish is flattened by bulldozers. Then heavy **compactors** with spiked wheels squash the rubbish even more. At the end of every day the rubbish is covered with a layer of earth to stop rats and flies getting into the waste.

Landfill sites have other problems. Water from rain or underground streams draining through the sites may mix with the poisonous liquids which are made as the rubbish breaks down. When this polluted water drains into streams and ponds it can harm wildlife.

Sometimes, instead of being buried, rubbish is burnt in large machines called **incinerators**. Huge magnets pick out any steel, tin or pieces of iron. These can be recycled. The rest of the rubbish is burnt to ash. The ash takes up only about 10 per cent of the space of the original rubbish and no longer attracts flies and rats. The ash can be used for making roads.

It is often better to burn rubbish than to bury it, but burning has its problems too. Incineration produces harmful gases and pollutes the air. Today there are strict rules about how rubbish should be burnt in incinerators.

Why not recycle it?

When you think about the huge amounts of rubbish we produce and the problems that can occur when we try to bury or burn it, it makes sense to reuse or recycle what we can. About 75 per cent of the rubbish produced could be reused or recycled.

In many parts of the world, people do not throw away so much rubbish. The people in countries such as India and China are more likely to try to reuse or recycle things.

These workers in Pakistan have found many different ways of using old rubber tyres. They turn the worn-out tyres into rubber buckets, and rubber soles for shoes.

Recycling means making new things from items that have been used and are not needed any more. The old newspapers in the picture can be broken down into a **pulp** and made into new paper goods such as cardboard and eggboxes. Glass jars can be melted down and made into new glassware. Waste food and plant material like the orange peel can be made into **compost** to spread on the soil in the garden. Only plastics are difficult to recycle at the moment because there are so many different kinds.

Sorting for recycling

Different kinds of rubbish are recycled in different ways. This means that rubbish must be sorted into different kinds of materials, such as metal, glass, paper, old clothes and plant waste.

In China, bottles are carefully sorted and put into wire baskets. Cardboard is folded flat and tied up in bundles ready for collection. This makes it much easier to collect the bottles and cardboard for recycling, especially when the rubbish is taken away on a bicycle.

Metals

Metal food and drink cans are probably made of either **steel** or **aluminium**. The two metals can be separated at home by a simple test. Put a magnet on the side of a can. The magnet will cling to a steel can. If it falls off, the can is aluminium, which is not magnetic.

It is easy to recycle aluminium. In the United States, 50 per cent of aluminium drinks cans are recycled. People sell huge sacks of aluminium cans to buyers who call regularly at convenient collecting points, like shopping centre car parks. Waste steel can be recycled and made into new cars, cookers and fridges.

Glass

Glass bottles and jars must be sorted by colour before they are recycled. Any tops should be removed first. **Bottle banks** and **recycling centres** have separate containers to help people sort out the different colours. The broken glass, or **cullet**, of each colour is melted down separately to make new glass of that colour.

Paper

Waste paper can be mixed with water and broken down by machine into pulp. This is similar to the wood pulp which is made from crushing trees. The pulp from waste paper is often used to make cardboard. Our picture shows cardboard being made from recycled paper in Bangladesh. The cardboard sheets are drying in the sun.

Old clothes

Good quality used clothes and blankets are always wanted by charities such as Oxfam. If the clothes are clean and in good condition, they can be sold to raise funds for the charity.

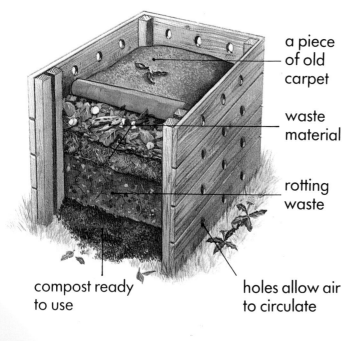

a piece of old carpet

waste material

rotting waste

compost ready to use

holes allow air to circulate

Plant waste

Quite a lot of rubbish from the kitchen is plant material. Cabbages and other vegetables usually need to have some of their outer leaves cut off before they are cooked. Banana and other fruit skins are put in the rubbish bin. This kind of rubbish can easily be collected in a separate container and then be used to make compost. When all the vegetable remains have been broken down, the compost can be put on the soil to help plants grow well. Most weeds and dead flowers from the garden can also be made into compost.

Plastics

In some places, plastics are collected for recycling. It is not easy to recycle plastics because the different kinds of plastic must first be sorted out. Mixed plastic cannot be used for recycling.

In Germany and some parts of the United States, you pay a **deposit** when you buy a full plastic bottle. When you take your empty plastic bottle back to the shop, you get the deposit back. This encourages people to return their empty plastic bottles and not just throw them away. The shops then return the bottles to the company that made them for refilling or recycling.

Recycling and energy

When goods are made in a factory, **energy** is needed to make machines work. Coal and oil are used to make heat energy and to make electricity in power stations.

Heat energy may be used to separate metals from their **ores**. The metals are used to make different kinds of goods. Electrical energy is needed to drive machines in factories. It generally takes less energy to make goods from recycled materials than to use **raw materials**.

It takes about twice as much energy to make paper from wood pulp as it takes to make recycled paper. Making aluminium from used drinks cans, like the ones in the photograph, takes only 5 per cent of the energy needed to extract aluminium from its ore.

Rubbish can be used to produce heat energy. **Methane** gas given off from rubbish in landfill sites can be burnt to produce heat energy. This energy can be used for warming homes and for making electricity.

Household waste can also be turned into **refuse derived fuel**, or **RDF**. This is made by cutting and crushing the rubbish into small pieces or pellets, like the ones in the photograph. The pellets can then be burnt to produce heat.

Heat from modern rubbish incinerators can be used to warm water and to produce energy to drive machines. All the rubbish collected in Disneyland in the USA is burned in an incinerator and the heat is used to make electricity. Denmark uses about 30 per cent of its household waste in this way to produce energy.

Recycling and the environment

Recycling rubbish is usually better for the environment than making goods from raw materials. The main ore used to make aluminium is bauxite. Most bauxite comes from tropical countries, where it is dug out of large surface mines. These mines destroy an enormous amount of land and look very ugly. It is easy to recycle aluminium. Recycling more aluminium would mean fewer bauxite mines and less destruction of the environment.

It takes about 17 trees to make one tonne of paper. Large areas of land are needed to grow trees for the huge amount of paper we use. Many people think that the **plantations** where the trees are grown do not look attractive because only one type of tree is planted. It is more interesting to see a variety of trees. The plantations also take up land that could be used for farming. If we recycle more paper we would need fewer plantations.

Power stations that burn oil or coal pollute the air with heavy smoke and fumes. These fumes mix with water vapour in the air to make acid rain.

In Germany and the United States, oil extracted from old worn-out rubber tyres is used as a fuel in some power stations. This kind of fuel causes less air pollution than burning coal.

What can you do?

Reduce your rubbish

Goods in shops often have lots of layers of wrappings. Chocolates may each be wrapped inside a box which is covered by a layer of plastic. When you buy the chocolates, the shop assistant usually puts them in a bag. Try to buy goods with as little wrapping as possible. The wrapping and bag not only add to the cost of the goods, but usually go straight into the rubbish bin.

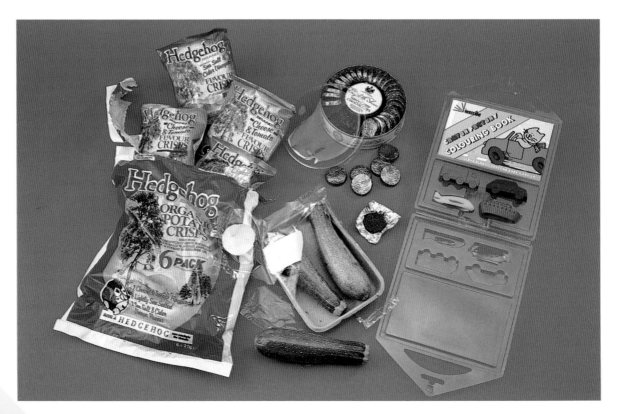

Another way to avoid instant rubbish is not to accept leaflets handed out in the street, or plastic bags provided free in supermarkets. Take your own bag when you go shopping and use it instead.

Today many goods are designed to be **disposable** and are meant to be used only once. Disposable nappies and disposable plates and glasses may be more convenient and save time, but they create yet more rubbish.

Whenever you can, buy good-quality goods that will last longer. A well-made toy is more likely to survive and be passed on to another child, than a poorly-made toy which will soon get broken and end up in the rubbish bin.

Reuse your rubbish

Some things, like plastic containers and glass jars, can easily be reused as long as they are not damaged and are made really clean. Many plastic bags can be reused, and most cardboard boxes as well.

Try to think of other uses for things you have finished with. A large cardboard box could be used as a playhouse for a younger brother or sister. Plastic yogurt and margarine tubs make good pots for growing seeds and small plants. You can probably come up with lots of other good ideas.

If you or your family have no way of reusing something, someone else may be grateful for it. Clothes and toys that you have grown out of but not worn out can be given to charity shops or jumble sales.

Recycle your rubbish

If you cannot reuse something, at least try to recycle it. If your rubbish for recycling is not collected separately, find out whether there is a recycling centre nearby. Your local supermarket car park may have a bottle bank where you can leave glass bottles and jars for recycling.

Whenever you can, buy things that are made from recycled materials. If people buy more recycled goods, firms will be more eager to make them. When you are using something that is recycled, encourage your friends to do the same.

23

Setting a good example

When you wonder what to do about your rubbish remember the three Rs: REDUCE, RECYCLE, REUSE. Try not to create so much rubbish in the first place. If you have something you no longer need, think about whether you can reuse it. If not, could it be recycled? Do not throw away anything until you are sure you cannot reuse or recycle it.

Some countries have laws about sorting out rubbish to encourage recycling. Some **councils** have door-to-door collection schemes for different kinds of rubbish.

REDUCE

RECYCLE   REUSE

People in the United States and some European countries are given a different coloured bin, or sometimes several different coloured bins, to sort their rubbish into. The sorted rubbish is collected by special rubbish trucks with separate compartments for the various kinds of rubbish. Sometimes each type of rubbish is collected on a different day. In Oregon, in the USA, if you do not sort your waste it will not be picked up!

In France, most supermarkets sell drinks in glass bottles that can be returned for refilling. In West Germany and the Netherlands, bottles for drinks are all made the same shape and size, whatever the contents. This makes reuse much easier. Shoppers take their crates of empty bottles back to the supermarket. The supermarkets then return the bottles to the **manufacturers** for refilling.

In Germany the government uses recycled paper to make some school books. As well as setting a good example, the off-white/grey paper makes people realize that good paper need not be white.

Activities

1 Make a survey of how many cans of soft drinks your friends drink each week. What do they do with the empty cans? Do they recycle them? If not, use the information you have collected to design a poster to encourage them to do so.

2 Ask your teacher to help you organize a recycling exhibition at your school. Collect as many things as you can that have been made from recycled materials. The picture shows some recycled goods. How many others can you find?

3 Make a chart with these headings:
Newspapers and magazines
Other paper and cardboard
Glass bottles and jars
Plastic bottles and jars
Plastic wrappings and bags
Metal tins and cans
Vegetable and fruit peelings
Other food scraps
Ask your family to keep a record of all the things they throw away in one week. Every time they put something in the bin, they should mark it on your chart. At the end of the week, ask them to see if they can reduce the amount a little next week.

Glossary

aluminium: a light, strong metal used to make many containers.

bottle bank: a container where empty glass bottles and jars can be left for recycling.

compactor: a machine which squashes things so that they take up less space.

compost: waste from leaves, grass-cuttings, and vegetable peelings broken down to make fertiliser for growing plants.

council: a group of people chosen by others living in the same area to look after the business of the area.

cullet: broken bits of glass used in the glassmaking process.

deposit: a small amount of money paid on something. The money is returned later if, for example, the bottle or container is returned to the shop.

disposable: made to be used once and then thrown away.

energy: the fuel necessary for work. People need food for energy. Machines need a fuel like electricity or petrol.

household: a family or group of friends who share the same house.

incinerator: a machine for burning rubbish.

landfill sites: large holes in the ground where rubbish is tipped and buried.

manufacturer: a company which makes goods.

methane: a gas which is given off when rubbish breaks down.

ore: a rock or mineral from which a useful metal can be obtained.

plantation: an area where a lot of trees of the same kind are being grown.

pollution: something which dirties or poisons the air, land, or water.

pulp: a wet, soft, mushy substance made from very small pieces of wood or paper and water.

quarry: a place where rocks and minerals are dug out of the ground.

raw materials: natural substances which are grown or taken out of the ground.

recycle: to make something new from something already used once.

recycling centre: a place where you can take materials such as paper, glass, cans, plastic and old clothes and put them into containers so that they can be recycled.

refuse derived fuel (RDF): small lumps of crushed rubbish which can be burnt to produce heat.

steel: a hard metal used to make knives, tools, machinery and containers.

tonne: a measurement of weight, equal to 100 kg.

Index